D1373394

LAS MEZCLADORAS DE CEMENTO
CEMENT MIXERS

Dan Osier

Traducción al español: Eida de la Vega

PowerKiDS
press.

New York

Published in 2014 by The Rosen Publishing Group, Inc.
29 East 21st Street, New York, NY 10010

First Edition

Editor: Amelie von Zumbusch
Book Design: Andrew Povolny   Traducción al español: Eida de la Vega

Photo Credits: Cover Zolwiks/Shutterstock.com; p. 5 Bram von Broekhoven/Shutterstock.com; p. 7 Baloncici/ Shutterstock.com; p. 9 Alistair Berg/Lifesize/Getty Images; p. 11 Hybrid Images/Cultura/Getty Images; p. 13 Dorling Kindersley/Getty Images; p. 15 Robert Pernell/Shutterstock; p. 17 upthebanner/Shutterstock.com; p. 19 imageegami/Shutterstock.com; p. 21 Andy Sotiriou/The Image Bank/Getty Images; p. 23 George Marks/Hulton Archives/Getty Images.

Library of Congress Cataloging-in-Publication Data

Osier, Dan.
 Cement mixers = Las mezcladoras de cemento / by Dan Osier ; translated by Eida de la Vega.
     pages cm. — (Construction site = En construcción)
 English and Spanish.
 Includes index.
 ISBN 978-1-4777-3289-2 (library)
 1. Concrete mixers–Juvenile literature. I. Osier, Dan. Cement mixers. II. Osier, Dan. Cement mixers. Spanish III. Title.
 IV. Title: Mezcladoras de cemento.
 TA439.O8518 2014
 629.225—dc23
                                        2013022464

Websites: Due to the changing nature of Internet links, PowerKids Press has developed an online list of websites related to the subject of this book. This site is updated regularly. Please use this link to access the list: www.powerkidslinks.com/cs/cement/

Manufactured in the United States of America

CPSIA Compliance Information: Batch # W14PK3: For Further Information contact Rosen Publishing, New York, New York at 1-800-237-9932

Contenido

Contents

Este camión es una
mezcladora de cemento.

This truck is a cement mixer.

Las mezcladoras de cemento cargan y mezclan **concreto**.

Cement mixers carry and mix **concrete**.

6

7

El concreto es una mezcla de cemento, agua, arena y piedritas.

Concrete is a mix of cement, water, sand, and small rocks.

8

El cemento es un polvo.
El cemento Portland es el más común.

Cement is a powder.
Portland cement is the most common kind.

11

El **tambor** del camión contiene el concreto.

The truck's **drum** holds the concrete.

12

13

El tambor gira. Esto impide que el concreto se ponga demasiado duro.

The drum spins around. This keeps the concrete from getting too hard.

15

El tambor gira hacia un lado para mezclar concreto y hacia el otro lado para verterlo.

Drums spin one way to mix concrete. They spin the other way to pour it.

El concreto se vierte por medio de **canaletas**.

The concrete is poured out through **chutes**.

Se endurece lentamente. Después de siete días, se pone completamente duro.

It gets hard slowly. It is fully hard after seven days.

Las mezcladoras de cemento se fabricaron por primera vez en Columbus, Ohio.

Cement-mixer trucks were first made in Columbus, Ohio.

BETTER SERVICE

COLONIAL
SAND & STONE CO., Inc.

CONCRETE
MIXED IN TRANSIT

CIRCLE 5·5400

331

SERVICE

COLONIAL

23

PALABRAS QUE DEBES SABER / WORDS TO KNOW

(la) canaleta

chute

(el) concreto

concrete

(el) tambor

drum